PRIDE OF A SCAR

Beauty radiates in different shades

It glows so brightly and sometimes so dimly

It tells a story in a million ways

Hidden beneath are tales the mouth wishes not to tell

Sometimes it refines us and also break us as well

It's warmth wrapped in the cold

This is beauty birthed from the ugly

Just as the moon radiates the light of the sun

And glows amid the stars

So does scar radiate its beauty

But through different shades

Some of betrayal, pain, sadness and defeat

Others of conquest, joy, vindication and prevail

There are unsung songs

That dance in the heart in victory or in shame

There are un-whispered secrets

That slips into the ears in contentment or in despair

As the air gives breath to life

So do a scar gives breath to experiences

ON THIS BED

On this bed, I lay

On Dreams that never had life

I'm a memory

That thrives on nostalgia

On this bed, I lay

Hallucinating on reality

In dreams filled with insomnia

Scared of my thoughts

These demons rage

On this bed, I lay

On dreams once filled with innocence

My desires ate up my humanity

I'm a body

Traversing on this plains filled with vultures

I'm pain locked in cells I built

To escape self-destruction

I became a ticking bomb

Hidden under a clock of innocence

I'm my own therapy

My doctor and my medication

That has preyed on me

It is easy to see my own reflection

In portraits and images that consumed me.

BETRAYED

He carved hate

His craving was governed by rage

Revenge for all the betrayal

That brought pain to his little hear, t now wild

So, he set out on a journey

To hunt all who fed on his vulnerability

This is the hour of payback

The wages are due for retribution

He growls in rage

This terror is the beginning of nemesis

Slung across his back is his chainsaw

And in his hand is an axe

To rip and hack down

All who taught him in the school of pain

What it meant to keep on living

When the inside was long dead

He razed the town

Making widows and orphans abound

In unbelievable numbers

The city lays in rumbles of its filth

Desolated in shame, pain and lament

Insatiable, has this urge overwhelmed him?

His reasoning is no longer humane The innocent boy has grown into a dreaded beast

His demons have overpowered his being

He grips his sword

With a hand

That once

Clung to his dad

He is on the run

Far away

From a place

He once called home

He finds solace in pain

Just like

He once found solace

In the bosom of his mother

He is an outcast

To a people

He once

Called family.

RAPE

Perverted thrust

She lost her Innocence

Even though her uncle claimed innocent

Only if she knew

Those little gifts and pettings were not free

Depression, a new song

Child of the world on a repeat

Hate, rooted in her young veins

Her heart no longer made for love

Raged profanity

Vowed vengeance

She slays on the streets of red lights

Her body refuse to be tamed

She desecrates every bed

A terror in every home

Wishful regrets

Drifting dreams

She settles down with the virus

Her dreams are now inverted

Gradually slipping into shadows

She lays, awaiting the final breath

REFLECTIONS

I'm a symbol of fading shadows

Sailing quietly on waves of wasted fantasies

It's dark in here

When you are all alone

In this journey of doom

Hopelessness is a name

Tagged on a lonely lad

Who wanted only to live

MEN ARE NOT STONES

I stand shoulder high

Not because I have never been down

Not because I have never been scared

Not because I have never doubted my fears

The darkest nights are always the shortest ones

I am only a naive boy

bred in a society where I have to look strong

They tell us men are the toughest

Never show emotions no matter the situations

So, we die inside to be a man.

OUTCAST

How do you write a thousand songs on the

lip of a cursed widow

Sadness is a companion that stays in her shadow

She is a reflection of a lost world

Written in a tag she never chooses

Don't tell her you feel her pain

For she is an outcast trodden by foot

Strange clouds besiege her existence

Her clock is for the forsaken

She is shadow in a body that is not hers.

HELLO

Hello from afar

Greetings I proclaim

To all new and old

Close and distant

How do I sleep

In dark and silence

Haunted by a prey

Cunning and harmless

Strange beholds mask

In beauty frozen

Endless fire brew

Tempting and healing

Listen to this silence

It's echo, overwhelming

Still as a stampede

Lifeless and serene

HOW NOT TO DIE

Our souls transverse on this lonely plains

We wander in this dark tunnel

Our shadows reminds us of our memories

How do we forget how to live?

Our tales have turned sour in our mouths

Our souls sails on this troubled waters

We drown in this sea of helplessness

Our reflections have been soiled

How do we forget how to die?

Our graves have been neglected by our bodies

In despair we forgot our roots

Planted on soil that gives life

We are sons of the soil

We don't die, we transit

We soar high

In skies that breaths freedom

For we are the stars

That illuminates the nights

SANITY

The night sleeps gently awake

Singing lullaby of lovely doom

I want to tell you my tale

This heart is heavy, it floats weightlessly

Grief wrap in glee

I love being sober while drunk

For I chatter in wise-fool silence

And I release my burden in captivity

What if I was too crazy while sane

What if I walked in a crowded path alone

What if I didn't make the choices I refused to choose

What if I was so weak while strong

What if I had a soft spot so hard to spot

What if these if's were not ifs

I chose to see

Colorful pictures

That are blank

In white and black

Let me be

I will be awake

When my sanity is restored.

JOURNEY OF REALITY

So Gloomy When I Try To See

Just Staring Makes Me Dizzy

The Journey So Far, yet Destination So Close

Fine World, yet Cruel Hearts

Never Let My Thoughts be Tamed

Still I Feel Untrue Calmness

Dashing Hopes From Unaccepted Trust

The Vision So Pure Yet Drowned In The Oceans

Brighter Sun Shaded By The Dark Clouds

When Feeling So Good Feels So Bad

Fairytale World I Dream To Live In

But The Fiery Flames Consumes Me With Reality

Imaginations Struck Hard

Still Answers To Why

Turns To Questions To How

Necessity Becomes A Useless Obsession

Wronging The Right

A Compulsory Precaution

An Invention To Evade This Premunition

Lost In The Speck Of Abjection

So I Set My Hope Haunting

Stumbling On Dreams Bumpers

To Shade These Ranting curses Of The Owl

Leaving My Footprints On This Coal Of Test

The Morrow Soon A Relief To Comfort

So I Let My Heart Soar On This Journey Of Truth.

I'M NOT A POET

I'm not a poet

Most times, my pen betray me while I write

Words I write while drunk

And I'm sober when blank

I'm not a poet

So I said,

In every piece penned

Putting my thoughts in symbols

that looks crazy to the sane mind

Guess this price I have to pay

for choosing to tow this lane

I'm not a poet

My world is crazy

I'm a victim

Of what I believe in

Can a Misfit be a poet? So they asked.

IF I COULD TAME THIS SCRIPT

If I Could Tame This Script,

Then My Pen Would Bleed For Man's Peril,

If Eden Could End This Chaos With Serenity,

Then Man's Fall Would Have Been Averted,

I Wish We All Had Bathed In The Pool Of Innocence,

Then The Scale Of Guilt Wouldn't have Fallen From Our Eyes,

Simplicity Have Turned So Complex,

Complex Have Caused So Much Agony,

Agony Have Lead To So Much Death,

And Death Could Have Save Much Lives,

If Only I Could Tame This Script,

My Tongue Have Lost Speech,

My Heart Is Clouded With Empty Vile Thoughts,

My Days Are No longer Exciting,

Dark Nights Trail This Journey,

And Man's Existence Is Mere Title For The Forsaken,

Tales Dread The Mouth,

And The Wise Hangs Wisdom Beneath The Soil,

Volumes Speak Enough Of Its Silence,

Till The Cock Crow To Tell Of A New Dawn,

I Sleep On This Bed Of Awful Lament.

ANGELS MOCKERY

Every Tear Receiving

In All Of This Mishappening

Jobs Are Misplacing

In This Cycle Of Malnutrition

Crime Is Waxing

The People Are Masking

Laments Stay Repeated

The Weak, Eliminated

Reality Inverted

The End Preceded

Tempted To Mistrust

Clearly Seen These Ills Thrusting

Agony, Multiplicative

Some Tranquil Emaciated

Dangling On This Thread Doom

Awaiting The Final Call

Night ended Lair

Where All The Forsaken Dwell

Dawn Dusk

Raising Cloud Musk

Misjudged Truth

Disdain Hurt

Nothing Left

Not Even The Heros Might

Angels Stars

Mockery Path

Dethroned Hope

Serpent Treat

Future Past

Present Seeking

Faith Extincting

Nerves, Somersaulting

Let The Foreseeable Be View

With An Eagle Eye

Soaring Above These Chaos

Into The Rainbow Of Colours

To Paint Every Colour With Love

So I Ink This Truth

To Spill The Ills Of Men...

Dedicated To All Who Are Facing The Storm.

TO A LOVE UNLOVED

It was a tale

That was hidden deep in the shelves

She was tamed wild

By emotions that were that of a Judas

The night was dead to live again

It was a tale

That was repeatedly denied a life

It was frozen and lacked a heart

There was no redemption for this damned soul

She was dead though she was still breathing

It was a tale

Only to be a song for the cursed

Misfortune was just another blessing

For the wise to be outsmarted by the fool

This was paradise for those who couldn't be saved

It was a tale

Don't get into my head

For this mind is toxic

Don't breathe its air

For many have died by this life

It was a tale

Too sad to know joy

It was a reward gained

For all the love that was lost in lust

It was an innocence stained

For love wasn't the way she thought it was

She was too naive to define her feelings

Caution was not her lucky portion

She drank too deep

Never realizing how fast she was lured into this trap

She was a victim of her passion

She only wanted to feel love

If only love could love her back.

WORDS OF WISDOM

Papa, please tell us of yesterday,

When the world was young and pure,

Tell us the story about how it was created,

Lead us to the cave upon which life first drew breath,

Refresh our Minds let us learn of its mysteries

Show us the palm oil that stained it's fingers,,

Bade farewell to this lake lost,

And Let's sojourn into this maze dungeon,

Mama, if the new became old,

And the tears became smiles,

If the night became day,

And the lies become truth,

If doom became redemption,

And rejection became acceptance,

Then only time will fly,

And we will live ageless,

Son, let me tell you a tale,

Open your mind and let me fill it with wisdom,

Let the lesson of this tale,

Guide you along life's journeys,

Here I stand between past and future,

Let me growl my failure,

And moan out my pain,

Feel this beat my anguished heart,

And lament at its shame,

Tell my story,

And let the world feed from it.,

Daughter, let not your beauty,

Build pride in your head,

Let me show you my grey hair,

From wisdom age,

See my sunken jaw,

And learn from my sage lips,

Look into my weak eyes,

And let me open your vision into future,

Hold my hand steady,

And let me lead you along memory road,

Fly not high,

Lest the sun feeds on your wings,

Fly not low,

Lest the hunters arrows hit you in the heart,

Let wisdom chose you foolishly,

And let your aching heart heal health,

Worry not worry,

So you may find peace even among pieces,

Guide against chaos,

Lest you become swallowed by it,

Build home with unity, peace, patience and love.

And let the laughter remind us of how we used to live.

EMPTY REFLECTIONS

So, I woke up feeling sad

Some say I am ungrateful for a new day

Why will I be?

When every day feels worse

Don't try to preach to me

I'm done listening to this gibberish

All hope I had has drained my will to fight

I see dark shadows of my image

This innocence pleads guilty

I tried hard to pretend it was a dream

But I'm so scared to fall asleep

I think I have found a new love

How come I never noticed?

How tasty sniper could be!

No one ever told me

Blowing up my brain could feel so good

I think I should dangle happily on this rope

Or should I slit this throat and gladly embrace this end?

There was a time

My life was not so complex

When I could try counting the stars in contentment

I never had to worry what the next moment could be like

All I knew was a bliss filled with merriment

Life was fair, so I thought.

I'm an empty reflection

Fading into the shadows

The end has come

I was brave till I dropped cold.

Depression is real and people are suffering in silence, dying in silence, this could have been averted if only we showed a little love, a little care, I hear people saying that everyone goes through life's problems and everyone should hold on to his kettle., it's high time we imbue that mentality of showing care to people around us, be kind in our words and let them know we can fight this battle together.

HOW NOT TO DIE

Our souls transverse on this lonely plains

We wander in this dark tunnel

Our shadows reminds us of our memories past

How do we forgot how to live

Our tales has turned sour in our mouths

Our souls sail on these troubled waters

We drown in this sea of helplessness

Our reflections have been soiled

How do we forget how to die?

Our graves have been neglected by our bodies

In despair, we forgot our roots

Planted on soil that gives life

We are sons of the soil

We don't die, we transit

Our soils can't be caged

We soar high

In skies that breathe freedom

For we are the stars

That illuminates the dark nights

HUMANITY MADE US HUMAN

How do I become the story that was never spoken of?

I seek peace in the turmoil that rages in my head

I seek silence in the distractions that besiege my eyes

I seek serenity from the words that continually haunt my soul

I was a young lad

Who only wanted to be different

Now I am different from the world I call home

I am a stranger in the land that gave life

I am an alien to the people that once called me brother

This poison has clouded our minds

It's a sore that never stops feasting on our eyes

It became the stain that dampened our souls

Teach me to live in a world that has lost its identity

Teach me to breathe life in a land that is losing how to live

Teach me to love in hearts that has been governed in rage

So, I pray to be free from all that made us lose our humanity.

IF I COULD TAME THIS SCRIPT

If I could tame this script

Then my pen would bleed for man's peril

If Eden could end this chaos with serenity

Then man's fall would have been averted

I wish we had all bathed in the pool of innocence

Then the scales of guilt wouldn't have fallen from our eyes

Simplicity have turned so complex

Complex have caused so much Agony

Agony have lead to so much deaths

And death could have save much lives

If only I could tame this script

My tongue have lost speech

My heart is clouded with empty vile thoughts

My days are no more exciting

Dark nights trail this journey

And man's existence is a mere title for the Forsaken

Tales dread the mouth

And the wise hangs wisdom beneath the soil

Volume speaks enough of its silence

Till the cock crow

To tell of a new dawn

I sleep on this bed

Of awful Lament.

LIFE AND THE TRUTH IT BRINGS

Inside of us

There lies a part

In our loneliest moments

There comes the truth

The less we pay attention to know

Then will the realization of what was missed be illumined

Sometimes,

It pays to seek less, hear less, and talk less

For in our wisdom,

We breed folly

Life feeds us with the food we desire not

To make us value what might have never been   valued

It brings us to our knees

To make us see our limitations and value its essence

It breaks us down

To build us up after a while

In what life dishes to us

Let's learn to trust its process and grow from it

For man's stability

Is determined by how solid its foundation.

LISTEN

Listen to this silence

It beckoned, we answered

Listen to this hunger

It's cravings, left us famished

Listen to this void

It's emptiness, made us helpless

Listen and hear

The oppression, injustice

Corruptions, killings

And all evils of men

Listen and see

The wickedness of man

It's deceptions and vile thoughts

It's anger and cruelty

Listen and act,

Then would

This silence be answered

This hunger's be satisfied

This void would be made full.

LOVE IS A SONG

Love is a song

It's beat thumps mildly at the heart

Listen to it's symphony

See how wildly it drives the feet to dance madly to it's tunes

Love is a song

Enjoy it's rhythm

Pluck this feeling

For its ripen

Suck at its fruits hungrily

And let it fill up this void

Sway gently in contentment

For this feeling has grown ripe

Tap gently in rhythm

Give life to this cold soul

Purge off its darkness

Feed it in love's diet

Watch as it takes its first step in love

Love is a song

Tap gently to it's rhythm

LOVE

Let's mould love

Let's give her wings to fly

Let's teach her to live her name

Let's colour her in white and red

Let's fan her to glow in radiance

Let's water her to grow up in beauty and health

Let's guard her from hate and all enemies that threatens her existence

Let's correct her when she goes wrong

Let's call her to solve war, poverty, hunger

And all that throws the world into chaos

Let's cuddle her and say sweet words to her ears

Let's comfort and assure her when she is in doubt

Let's spread her virus to contaminate the hearts of men

And bring infectious smiles to the lips of all

Who come in contact with her

Let's breath her to give life to this dying soul

MAN'S EMPTY SOUL

Search me

For I am an empty soul

Lost in the chaos of the world

I feel no longer at home

In this lowly plains

Filled with vultures

How do I see in this darkness that claims to be light?

How do I feed this hunger, so consuming

How do I quench this flames that destroy?

Life wasn't so complex or so I thought

I see shadows stripped off bodies

There is a similar grievance here

For these images have gone sour

Man is a lost lad cut off

In his search

He became empty

And lost the way

He became a reflection that's haunted

He tripped and was swallowed

Until he who was to redeemed took Flesh.

MY PRAYER

I seek courage to face the fears in the world

Where troubles toss all into this sea of misery

So I pray

Give me a mind

That I always think of goodness in everyone

Give me eyes

That I may see perfection in God's creations

Give me ears

That I may listen with compassion and act accordingly

Give me nose

That I may perceive God's greatness in his creatures

Give me arms

That I may help the needy and the poor

Give me a heart

That I may feel the sincere needs of all

Give me legs

That I may lead the vulnerable and the oppressed

It's time for us all to make a change and start living.

ON MY FATHER'S SHOULDER

Even if I fall a million times

Even if I fail a thousand times

Even if I am told I'm a failure, tens of times

Even if I am too weak to try just once more

I am not alone in this struggle

Though it may seem dark

And the light must have lost its shine

Still, I'm not scared

For I can overcome every mountains

'Cos I am standing tall on my father's shoulder...

OVERWHELMING

Does it rain when we cry?
Does the sky turn grey when grief rings ?
Does the sun hide behind the gloom?

How do we get broken so easily?
How do we mask this pain, so tormenting?
How do we forge strength from this thing called weakness?

How did we become so flawed ?
How did we become *the fault in our stars?*
How did we become the hand that extinguished this flame?

When did we grow so cold?
When did the stars became so gloomy?
When did we forget how to live?

Sadness is a companion that clings to my shadow?

Angry nights chasing naive strangers

For strange clouds besiege this existence

Listen to this silence

It's echo overwhelming

Still as a stampede

Lifeless and serene

Let me be

I will be awake

When sanity is restored.

SAY ME A PRAYER

Say me a prayer

When my knees get so weak

Sometimes, I doubt my faith

I see the tears and the pains

How do I untag this cloak of despair?

How do I undrink?

From what was never meant to be drunken with

Say me a prayer

For my vision is so clouded

Angry nights chasing naïve strangers

Loneliness crept in like a companion

And invaded the hearts of men

The dark came and man tripped

Say me a prayer

That I may see the sun

And blossom and radiate beauty

Say me a prayer

That I may have the courage

To untangle from this Web of fear

Say me a prayer

For I see hunger in the souls of men

The rejections, frustrations, anger and pain

Say me a prayer

That mankind may be restored to serenity

Say me a prayer

Say for us this prayer.

REDEMPTION

Just like the sun

It rose and shone forth

After the rain comes forth a rainbow

Despair was a garment mankind wore

The way was lost when the light grew dim

Uncertainty bred fear

And fear brought chaos

Man was clouded with vile thoughts

But this wasn't the end

The rain came

Just like a flower it sprouted

And brought beauty to the hearts of men

Redemption was near

A new light shines forth

To clear the doubts of man

What was promised took flesh

To bring back life that had been taken

When man slipped and fell.

SLEEP OH YOUNG ONES

Sleep, Oh Young Ones, For the days Have Become Nights

The Cradle Of Origin Has Turned the Beginning Of the End

Sowing On This Plain Of Tears

I See Innocent Children Holding On To The Arms Of Their Terrified Parents.

Sleep, Oh Young Ones For the days Have Become Nights

Every Joy Has Turned Lamentations,

Every Smile Has Turned Agony,

Every blessing Has Turned Misfortune,

Wailing On This Bed Of Pain

Waiting For the Morrow Light To Shine

Another Beginning Of Salvation

For The Beautiful Hearts Are Yet To Be Given Flesh.

Sleep, Oh Young Ones

For the days Have Become Nights

For the Tale Of The Night

Have Become The Songs Of Men

For the Beauty Of Harmony

Is Now the discord Of Enmity

For the days Are Empty,

For the skies Are Cloudy,

For this Breaths Are Scanty,

Drink From this Lake Of Pain

And Let The Brightened Dark Lead the Way

Never Again Will this Laughter Be Seen

For All Has Fallen Apart

And *The Centre Can No Longer Take Its Hold.*

Sleep, Oh Young Ones

That Ye May Not See The Woes Of Men

For The Tragedy Of This Tale Will Become the Wisdom Of Tomorrow

THE FALL

It hovered slowly

Then it came to the dust

And gave it a body

It came into the body

And gave it life

Life was in its pure form

And lived in splendor and serenity

Then came another,

An intruder,

It planted a seed

On dust that had become the body

And body that had been breathed in life

This seed grew

And became a mighty tree

With many kinds of fruits

And when life tasted these fruits

It became a body

And this body

Then became dust again.

TO ALL I EVER CHERISHED

To all I ever cherished

How do I break these memories off this wall?

It gets a bit lonely in here

How do I trace my way back home?

I was consumed with an obsession

And became a shadow that reflects sad tales

It was innocent

I became drawn in

And was enchanted by its spell

Now I am a prisoner to my desires

Desires that stripped me off my innocence

Would you blame me for wanting more of good possessions?

Would you judge me for being my victim?

I drink too deep now

I'm drowning in this sea of cares

I'm chocking by this breath that once gave comfort

I'm tangled in this web called greed

Life was simple

Simple became boring

Then I made it exciting

Exciting turned complex

Now I am a captain

Captain Of exciting complexities.

THINKING OUT LOUD

Simple Life, complicated Dreams

Just An Ambition

A Little Hesitation

Bitter Truth, soothing Lies

Just My Agility

No Need For Ability

Clever Mind, foolish Wisdom

I Never Make Mistakes

Why Should My Flaws Be Seen

Reality Versus Favoured Assumptions

Deception Versus True Identity

When I Remember What I Remember

Marks Of Freedom

From Slavery Chains

Just A Dream

Long Forgotten

David's Victory

Job's Trials

Joy Of Sadness

Lamentation of Euphoria

Oh When My Heart Ache

For What I Should Have Done

Rather Than What I Have Done

When Haunting Hunt

Feast Feasting Loot

Terror Strikes

Titans Assembly

Medusa Lair

Vampires Convoy

Till Fear Turns Care

And Care Turns Cheer

Let Me Be

Until Comfort Embrace Empathy

And Forgiveness Is Derived from Mercy

So My Ink Flows

For All These ills Bleeding

Lives More Ending

From All These Swords Killings

Most Hearts Crushed

From All These Evil Cursed

This End, from Beginning Doom

Weavers Loom

From a Funeral Hum

Twinkle Stars Send My Shooting Star

So I Can Wish Upon Many Dreams.

THE WORD

It was a word

And it conceived

And birthed life

It was a promise

And it became fulfilled

At an appointed time

Man was lone, lost, and feeble

Weakened by his fall

Then distractions came

And man lost direction and focus

Then came redemption

Through a word

As promised by the creator

And mankind was connected

Once again back to life

At its fulfilment at the appointed time.

THE NIGHT WAS COLD

The night was cold

It froze the stars

The sky was silent

As the sun went to sleep

The wind whispered lazily

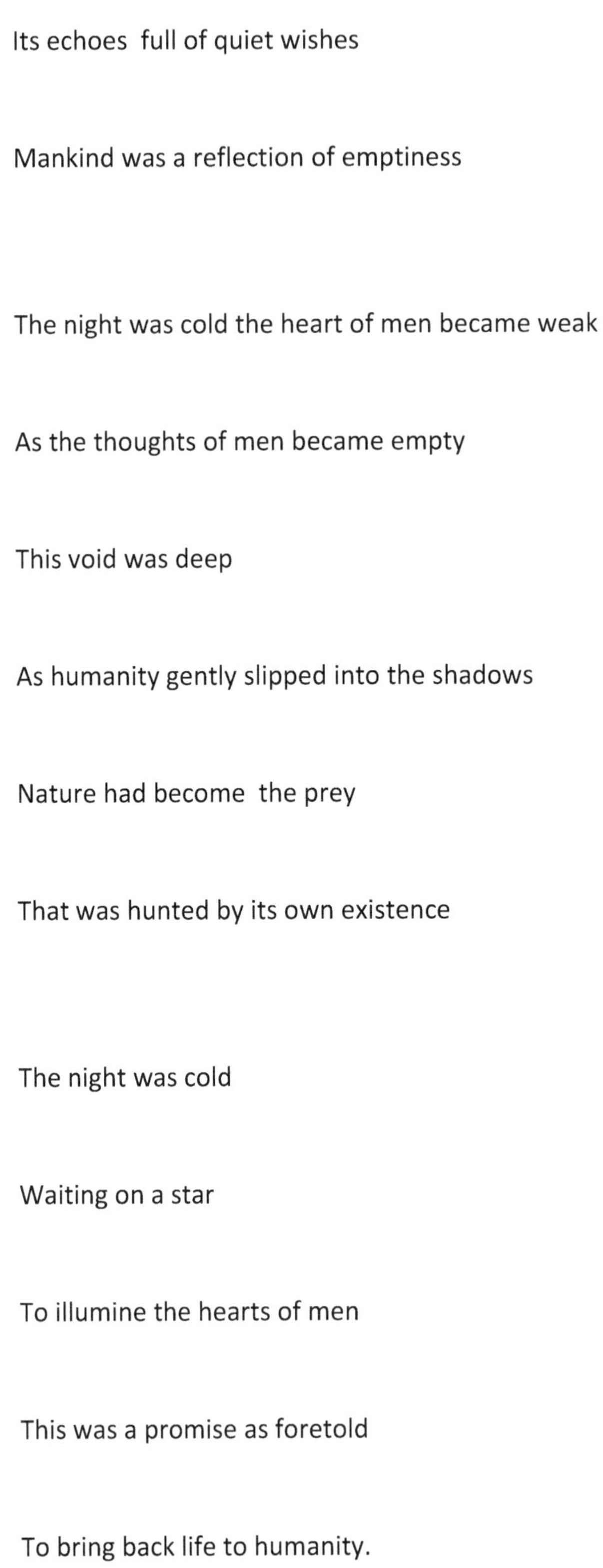

Its echoes full of quiet wishes

Mankind was a reflection of emptiness

The night was cold the heart of men became weak

As the thoughts of men became empty

This void was deep

As humanity gently slipped into the shadows

Nature had become the prey

That was hunted by its own existence

The night was cold

Waiting on a star

To illumine the hearts of men

This was a promise as foretold

To bring back life to humanity.

THE STARS LEAD THE WAY

Listen it calls deep

Don't stray from this path

The journey is exhausting

Fear blows calmly

Listen, it beckons close

Don't stop your ear from hearing itsit's voice

The journey is distracting

Anxiety waves calmly

Listen, it whispers in the wind

Don't stop to take rest

The journey is frustrating

Perplexity rings calmly

Listen carefully

Don't get lost

The journey is confusing

But the Stars lead the way.

SING ME A SONG

Sing me a song

That I may float weightlessly in thoughts

Comfort my troubled heart

That I may heal ache

Let me see the beauty of the world

That I may radiate joy

What is the sky

Without the sun, moon, stars, clouds, wind, and birds

What is the soil

Without the plants, animals, and man

What is the sea,

Without the fishes, and sea mammals

What is the universe,

Without the earth and the life it breeds

I choose to sing a song

That will make me float above my burdens

I choose comfort

That will heal this heart torn by worries and pains

I choose to see

The colors of the rainbow in the world
that radiates its splendor

So I say

Sing me a song

To comfort this troubled heart

That I may see the beauty of the world

And radiates its joy.

SHE SMILED

She Smiled And All Wars Were Ended

She Smiled And Hearts Of Stones Had Flesh

She Smiled And The Sufferings Of Men Vanished

She Smiled And Everything Became New Again

She Smiled And I Also Became Infected With Laughter...

WHEN DOVES CRY

Picture this

I'm young and innocent

Told a woman's pride

Is in her spotlessness

Fairy tale fantasies

Wrapped around my head

Could it be in the sitting room

Or probably in between the white sheets

Hope he won't be disappointed

Hope the stories he hears

Gladdens his heart

Hope this innocence

Would build up this pride and worth

Tell him how much I love him

Let him see this affection in our gaze

Tell him how I save this up for him

Let this bond be the beginning of trust

Tell him I have been faithful to this love

Let him be true to this love declared

Never wanted much for me

I dreamt only of a simple home

Why is this world so cold

Could fate be this cruel

Is this how this pride will become humiliated

How come this innocence is now stained?

Could it be I was too demanding?

Maybe I was engulfed in keeping my worth

Maybe I was never satisfied

Maybe I closed my eyes to harsh realities

Maybe I stumbled and fell too quick

Maybe I became so lonely in my fantasies

Now this worth is worthless

This pride has become humiliated

My innocence hovers around guilt

If only I trod with caution

This new burden would never have surfaced

Now I'm a shadow of my past

Trailing this lane filled with anguish

I now know how it feels

When doves cry.

www.ingramcontent.com/pod-product-compliance
Lightning Source LLC
Chambersburg PA
CBHW040947110726
48006CB00007B/1288